# Whale Day

AND OTHER POEMS

*Billy Collins*

RANDOM HOUSE

NEW YORK

LIBRARY OF CONGRESS CATALOGING-IN-PUBLICATION DATA
Names: Collins, Billy, author.
Title: Whale day : and other poems / Billy Collins.
Description: First edition. | New York : Random House, [2020] |
Identifiers: LCCN 2020003903 (print) | LCCN 2020003904 (ebook) |
ISBN 9780399589775 (trade paperback) | ISBN 9780399589768 (ebook)
Subjects: LCGFT: Poetry.
Classification: LCC PS3553.O47478 W48 2020 (print) |
LCC PS3553.O47478 (ebook) | DDC 811/.54—dc23
LC record available at https://lccn.loc.gov/2020003903
LC ebook record available at https://lccn.loc.gov/2020003904

Printed in the United States of America on acid-free paper

randomhousebooks.com

4 6 8 9 7 5 3

Title-page and part-title images: © iStockphoto.com

*Book design by Dana Leigh Blanchette*

## BY BILLY COLLINS

*Musical Tables*

*Whale Day*

*The Rain in Portugal*

*Aimless Love: New and Selected Poems*

*Horoscopes for the Dead*

*Ballistics*

*The Trouble with Poetry and Other Poems*

*Nine Horses*

*Sailing Alone Around the Room:*
*New and Selected Poems*

*Picnic, Lightning*

*The Art of Drowning*

*Questions About Angels*

*The Apple That Astonished Paris*

## EDITED BY BILLY COLLINS

*Bright Wings: An Illustrated Anthology*
*of Poems About Birds*
(illustrations by David Allen Sibley)

*Poetry 180: A Turning Back to Poetry*

*180 More: Extraordinary Poems for Every Day*

# Whale Day

*For Laura,*
*treasured friend and patron*

"No one has a right to say that no water babies exist till they have seen no water babies existing, which is quite a different thing, mind, from not seeing water babies."

—CHARLES KINGSLEY

# Contents

## TWO

## THREE

# FOUR

# Whale Day

## The Function of Poetry

I woke up early on a Tuesday,
made a pot of coffee for myself,
then drove down to the village,
stopping at the post office
then the bank where I cashed a little check
from a magazine, and when I got home
I read some of the newspaper
starting with the science section
and had another cup of coffee and a bowl of cereal.

Pretty soon, it was lunchtime.
I wasn't at all hungry
but I paused for a moment
to look out the big kitchen window,
and that's when I realized
that the function of poetry is to remind me
that there is much more to life
than what I am usually doing
when I'm not reading or writing poetry.

# One

# Walking My Seventy-Five-Year-Old Dog

She's painfully slow,
so I often have to stop and wait
while she examines some roadside weeds
as if she were reading the biography of a famous dog.

And she's not a pretty sight anymore,
dragging one of her hind legs,
her coat too matted to brush or comb,
and a snout white as a marshmallow.

We usually walk down a disused road
that runs along the edge of a lake,
whose surface trembles in a high wind
and is slow to ice over as the months grow cold.

We don't walk very far before
she sits down on her worn haunches
and looks up at me with her rheumy eyes.
Then it's time to carry her back to the car.

Just thinking about the honesty in her eyes,
I realize I should tell you
she's not really seventy-five. She's fourteen.
I guess I was trying to appeal to your sense

of the bizarre, the curiosities of the sideshow.

I mean who really cares about another person's dog?

Everything else I've said is true,

except the part about her being fourteen.


I mean she's old, but not that old,

and it's not polite to divulge the true age of a lady.

# Contemporary Americans

I was trying to make my way
across a busy street in San Francisco,
while carrying the new anthology of poetry
I'd been flipping through earlier that morning—
with my pot of tea and two pieces of cinnamon toast—
in which I was wedged between James Tate and Bob Dylan
because the poets were arranged old to young, according to age.

I had to avoid a couple of cars,
cross over two sets of trolley tracks,
and dodge a guy with a ski cap on a bicycle
in order to get across the street and enter
one of the city's many hospitable parks
with their hedges, benches, and shade trees
and often girls on a blanket, a juggler, an old man doing tai-chi.

And that's where I lay down on the soft grass,
closed my eyes, and after a little while
began to picture the three of us lined up in a row
according to the editor's wishes,
sliding out of our mothers in order, one after the other,
then ending up pressed together on a shelf
in a corner bookstore, yodeling away in the dark.

## Paris in May

A teddy bear in a store window,
three housepainters
waiting to cross a boulevard,
a woman in a café, her red nails
on a man's nape while she smokes—
what are we to make of all this?

In the church of Saint-Sulpice,
the Virgin holds her baby to her chest
as she stands on the round earth,
appearing to be unaware
of the serpent she is crushing with one foot.
Outside, four stone lions guard a fountain.

Is this a puzzle I am meant to solve
before the evening bells ring again—
here a man wearing a newspaper hat,
there a child alone on a flowery balcony?
An outdoor table on Rue Cassette
seemed a good enough place to sort things out.

And sure enough,
after two milky-green glasses of Pernod,
the crowd flowed around me like a breeze,
and I found a link between my notebook
and the soft Parisian sky,
both being almost the same pale shade of blue.

# And It's Raining Outside, Which Always Adds

About a month ago, I bought a small transistor radio in a junk shop
run by a man as tall as a grandfather clock,
a pink plastic one from the nineteen fifties,
which plays only love songs from the past,
as if the radio had a memory and a melancholy disposition.

I like to turn the little bezel with my thumb
so the volume is down so low, the songs
sound as if they're coming from another room
in a boardinghouse in a run-down part of town.
Then I lie down and lock my hands behind my head.

Tonight, "They Say It's Spring"
is making all the boarders in the boardinghouse sad,
but that's the way it is with every song,
whether it's "April in Paris" or "Autumn in New York,"
which were both written by the same guy,

but the boarders are too unhappy to care about that,
the men sitting on the edges of their beds,
and the women looking out the only window at the rain
where a taxicab as yellow as forsythia is turning a corner
to God knows where and God knows who,

and God knows why "You Go to My Head" is playing now,
bringing down all the poor souls in the boardinghouse,
which vanished when I heard someone speak and opened my eyes.

## Life Expectancy

On the morning of a birthday that ended in a zero,
I was looking out at the garden
when it occurred to me that the robin
on her worm-hunt in the dewy grass
had a good chance of outliving me,
as did the worm itself for that matter
if he managed to keep his worm-head down.

It was not always like this.
For decades, I could assume
that I would be around longer
than the squirrel dashing up a tree
or the nightly raccoons in the garbage,
longer than the barred owl on a branch,
the ibis, the chicken, and the horse,

longer than four deer in a clearing
and every creature in the zoo
except the elephant and the tortoise,
whose cages I would hurry past.
It was just then in my calculations
that the cat padded noiselessly into the room,
and it seemed reasonable,

given her bright eyes and glossy coat,

to picture her at my funeral,

dressed all in black, as usual,

which would nicely set off her red collar,

some of the mourners might pause in their grieving to notice,

as she found a place next to a labradoodle

in a section of the church reserved for their kind.

## Sleeping on My Side

Every night, no matter where I am
when I lie down, I turn
my back on half the world.

At home, it's the east I ignore,
with its theaters and silverware,
as I face the adventurous west.

But when I'm out on the road
in some hotel's room 213 or 402
I could be pointed anywhere,

yet I hardly care as long as you
are there facing the other way
so we are defended in all degrees

and my left ear is pressing down
as if listening for hoofbeats in the ground.

## The Floors of Bonnard

Surely the slanted tables are responsible
for all the shattered crockery,
the puddles of wine, and the clumps of butter
that must end up on the rarely seen floors
in the colorful paintings of Pierre Bonnard.

Tilting the table forward in the direction
of the viewer is one way
to make more visible the red-orange tablecloth

and all the objects resting on it:
the plates and saucers, the creamer,
wineglasses, vases, and delicate teacups.

But what about the poor wife of Bonnard?
Why is she never glimpsed
amidst all the colorful fabrics,
reds, pale blues, and vermillion dots,
bearing her broom, her dustpan, and her putrid mop?

## Down on the Farm

Whenever the conversation turns to the subject
of Tennessee Fainting goats,
the question that always comes up is why.
Are they so squeamish that they faint
like Victorian ladies whenever the farmer
uses language unbecoming a gentleman?

Or is it catching, one goat fainting
because he sees another one fainting,
but that still leaves open the question
of what makes the first goat faint.
Does the memory of having keeled
over one morning make one keel over again?

Are they in love? Or is it all just too much?
No one seems to know for sure
but it's something to think about
when I'm trying to get to sleep at night
or when I'm looking out a window
at the barn and the fenced-in pastures beyond.

To see a goat stiffen before pitching over on its side
with a thump is truly unnerving,
but when he rises in a minute or two, as if from the dead,
and goes back to munching with his head down
in the sweet grass on these hillsides,
then everything seems okay again, just like before.

## Imperial Garden

It was at the end of dinner,
the two of us in a red booth
maintaining our silence,
when I decided to compose a message
for the fortune cookie you were soon to receive.

*Avoid mulishness when choosing*
*a position on the great board game of life*

was my mean-spirited contribution
to the treasury of Confucian wisdom.

But while we waited for the cookies,
the slices of oranges,
and the inescapable pot of watery tea,
I realized that by *mulishness*
I meant your refusal to let me
have my own way every time I wanted it.

I watched you looking off to the side—
your mass of dark hair,
your profile softened by lamplight—
and then I made up a fortune for myself.

*He who acts like a jerk*
*on an island of his own creation*
*will have only the horizon for a friend.*


I seemed to be getting worse at this,
I thought, as the cookies arrived at the table
along with the orange slices
and a teapot painted with tigers
menacingly peering out from the undergrowth.


The restaurant was quiet then.
The waiter returned to looking out at the street,
a zither whimpered in the background,


and we turned to our cookies,
cracking the brittle shells,
then rolling into little balls
the tiny scrolls of our destinies
before dropping them, unread, into our cups of tea—
a little good-luck thing we'd been doing ever since we met.

## Mice

I was normally alone in my childhood,
a condition that gave me time
to observe the activities of the many mice
that had infested our house
one winter night when the house
next door burned to a crisp.

They all ran across the snow-
covered lawn to find places
to hide in their new home;
then later they discovered the kitchen,
which was like Columbus discovering
America, because the kitchen was already there.

I became their only spectator
like someone alone in a movie house.
I could even tell some of them apart,
but I resisted giving them names,
afraid they would all disappear
if our house happened to burst into flames.

O, anonymous companions,
appearing in a hole in the wall,
always scurrying out of my reach,
so many hours I would watch
your comings and goings,
before someone called me down to dinner;

you were the beginning of cinema for me
and one of the reasons
I am the way I am this morning—
an elderly child with a tummy
full of oatmeal and a mouse on my shoulder,
standing on its hind legs, whispering in my ear.

## Prospect

I'm high up
on a kitchen chair
so I can reach

a clear glass vase
to put some flowers in
and just to have a look around.

From up here everything
is an aerial drawing
of a kitchen, with the sink, the stove,

and the tall refrigerator
conveying a plummeting sensation
as if all their vertical lines ended in hell.

Yes, I'm getting a slightly different
sense of things from up here
but that's really about it. In fact,

I wouldn't recommend this to anyone.
Chances are you will feel silly
standing on a chair in the kitchen

once you finished whatever
it was you climbed up there to do—
a far cry from the originality

of Petrarch, grandfather of the sonnet,
who is thought to be
the first person in known history

to ascend a mountain
to the very top
just for the sake of the view.

## Evening Wind

is the title of one of Edward Hopper's
pen-and-ink drawings,
which I spent some time looking at
in a gallery on the far west side of town.

Hopper could have called it
*Totally Naked Woman Crawling*
*on All Fours into an Unmade Bed*
for she does occupy the foreground fully,

so it was only later that I noticed
the curtains behind her being lifted
by what must be an evening wind.
Then I noticed that the woman appears

to be looking at those curtains,
her face hidden by the dark curtain of her hair.
Or is she looking through the curtains
at the jagged outline of the city buildings,

topped with water tanks in silhouette?
It was not until I closed my eyes and imagined
her gradually falling asleep
after sliding naked under the covers

that I could envision the evening wind,

not just the wind as revealed by the curtains,

but the invisible wind itself blowing

through the room of this ingeniously titled drawing.

## Whiskers

I'm in a large brown armchair
sipping an espresso from a tiny cup,
and with the other hand
I'm stroking the whiskers on my face,
the ones that grew while I was asleep,
a night's worth of whiskers
and proof of my continuing existence.

Samuel Johnson refuted the position
of the great philosopher
Bishop (George) Berkeley
on the existence of material objects
by kicking him in the head,
if my historical memory serves,
but all I need is a face full of whiskers.

The whiskers of Dr. Johnson (1709–1784)
are no more, likewise the Bishop's (1685–1753),
but mine keep lengthening
night and day every day and night,
one amazing millimeter at a time,
and no brutal assault on a clergyman
is needed to prove the daily surprise of my being.

## *Walking Under the Trees*

I'm walking under the trees
walking in and out of their shadows
walking step by step under the trees
so the leaves on their lowest branches
graze my bare head
as I walk slowly under the trees
so close to me they could have
their arms around my shoulders,
walking under the guardian trees.

I'm walking under the trees
plucking a leaf
and putting it in my pocket
so I won't forget walking
under the cloak of these trees
thinking of nothing else
but the trees and me walking
under all their leaves and branches
walking all morning under the trees.

## Whale Day

Today I was awakened by strong coffee
and the awareness that the earth is busy with whales
even though we can't see any
unless we have embarked on a whale watch,
which would be disappointing if we still couldn't see any.

I can see the steam rising from my yellow cup,
the usual furniture scattered about,
and even some early light filtering through the palms.

Meanwhile, thousands of whales are cruising
along at various speeds under the seas,

crisscrossing one another, slaloming in and out
of the Gulf Stream, some with their calves
traveling alongside—such big blunt heads they have!

So is it too much to ask that one day a year
be set aside for keeping in mind
while we step onto a bus, consume a ham sandwich,
or stoop to pick up a coin from a sidewalk

the multitude of these mammoth creatures

coasting between the continents,

some for the fun of it, others purposeful in their journeys,


all concealed under the sea, unless somewhere

one breaks the surface

with an astonishing upheaval of water

and all the people in yellow slickers

rush to one side of the boat to point and shout

and wonder how to tell their friends about the day they saw a whale?

# Two

# The Wild Barnacle

*Do not speak, wild barnacle, passing over this mountain . . .*

—PATRICK PEARSE

In a lullaby by the Irish poet Patrick Pearse,
a woman of the mountain begins
singing her baby to sleep
by asking Mary to kiss her baby's mouth
and Christ to touch its cheek,
then she gets busy quieting the world around her.

All the grey mice must be still
as well as the moths fluttering
at the cottage window lit by the child's golden head.

Then, amazing to me—
one summer night when I first read the poem—
she orders a barnacle, of all things,
not to speak as it passes over a mountain.
To me, a barnacle came with a shell,
lived underwater, and stayed put
after silently affixing itself to a rock,
but here in the hands of a poet,

the small creature is miraculously
endowed with the powers of speech and flight.

I could see it now on a mountaintop,
its black shell shiny with salt water,
no more than two inches tall,
but dancing and riotous with joy and rage,
shouting the anthem of the barnacle,
loud enough to wake up
every baby in Connemara and beyond.

But, of course, it is the barnacle goose
that Pearse had in mind, I later found out,
common in the west of Ireland
and quite capable of flight with a honk
that could possibly alarm a sleeping baby.

For a moment, I had my own wild barnacle,
but the barnacle goose is fact,
and so is the fact that Patrick Pearse,
known as the schoolmaster,
was the one who proclaimed the independence of Ireland
from the steps of the General Post Office,

and for his troubles he was stood up
with fourteen other insurrectionists—
save Connolly who was seated
due to a recently shattered ankle—

yes, was stood up against the fact of a wall,
in a courtyard of Kilmainham Gaol, Dublin,
and executed by a British firing squad
in his final May in the terrible, beautiful year of 1916.

## Objectivity

Call it a compulsion, but every time
I give someone a new poem to look at,

I feel compelled to hide somewhere
and read that poem
as if I were that other person.

Pretending to be someone else
brings a new sense of objectivity,
revealing the poem's many flaws,
and suddenly makes me aware
of the pointlessness of having written it
and the sheer vanity of the entire enterprise.

Sometimes,
such a clarification may occur
without the help of another person,

but then I don't experience the relief
that comes from no longer
being me, if only for the time
it takes to read a poem on a single page.

Then I'm George, or Art, or even Suzannah,
none of whom wrote that poem;
thus I am able to read it
as if for the first time,
as if I'd never written it,

as if no one had ever written it for that matter,
as if I were not acquainted
with anyone named George, Art, or Suzannah.

Now there is no poem, and no more me,
yet here I am, swaying
in the hammock of my nonexistence.

But after only a few ticks of this,
I'm back in the room where I write
and back on my old schedule—
the tartan cover lifted from the grindstone,
boot on the foot treadle,
nose lowering to the task.

## Banana School

The day I learned that monkeys
as well as chimps, baboons, and gorillas
all peel their bananas from the other end
and use the end we peel from as a handle,
I immediately made the switch.

I wasted no time in passing this wisdom on
to family, friends, and even strangers
as I am now passing it on to you—
a tip from the top, the banana scoop,
the inside primate lowdown.

I promise: once you try it
you will never go back except
to regret the long error of your ways.

And if you do not believe me,
swing by the local zoo some afternoon
with a banana in your pocket
and try peeling it in front of the cage
of an orangutan or capuchin monkey,

and as you begin, notice
how the monkeys stop what they're doing,
if they are doing anything at all,
to nod their brotherly approval through the bars.

Better still, try it out on the big silverback gorilla.
See if you can get his dark eyes to brighten a bit
as the weight of him sits there in his cage
the same way Gertrude Stein is sitting
in that portrait of her she never liked by Picasso.

# *Identity*

Shortly after it was discovered
that Homer was not the author
of the *Iliad* or the *Odysssey*,
that, in fact, the *Iliad* was written
by another poet of the time named Homer
while the source of the *Odyssey*
remained unclear,
it was also discovered that God
did not create the universe.

It turns out that the creator
of this whole mishmash
was the identical twin brother of God,
even though no one in heaven
had ever been able to tell them apart,
even on weekends, when they
never wore the same outfit.

Does this mean that in the future
no one will know the difference
between a raven and a crow
or John Adams from John Quincy Adams?
and that you and I

will not be able to recognize one another?
That would be horrible,
plus, I would hate that
because I so much enjoy dining with you
and going on car trips with you navigating,

not to mention the pleasure
of sleeping in the same bed with you
with the backs of our heads
and the soles of our feet touching

so that we'd look like a giant arrowhead
if we ever became visible from space,
like smoke from a vast fire or the Great Wall of China.

## Arizona

In the marbled silence of the desert
it's easy to pick out the songs of birds,
which puts me in a better state of mind
than the one I wake up to some mornings
as I lie in bed worrying about the same five things
I will still be worried about on my deathbed
if I am lucky enough to have a deathbed
and not a tall death-wave or a deep death-lake
or a dizzying death-cliff, a death-gun or a death-knife,
and death is only one of the five nightly hounds
that prowl in circles around my bed.

And so, you birds of Arizona,
I am lucky to spend this time with you
amid the amber rocks and sudden wildflowers
to listen to your sweet mix of songs,
sorry I am not as knowledgeable as the woman
who just hurried past me up the switchback trail
with her binoculars and her bird book,
but grateful for the perfect acoustics
of your company in the lowering heat,
knowing that in mornings to come
I might recall that you and I were truly here.

## Irish Spider

It was well worth traveling this far
just to sit in a box of sunlight
by a window in a cottage

with a steaming cup of tea
and to watch an Irish spider waiting
at the center of his dewy web

pretending to be just any spider at all—
a spider without a nation—
but not fooling me for a minute.

*Listening to Hank Mobley Around 11 O'Clock*
*After a Long Fun Boozy Dinner, the Four of Us,*
*at Captain Pig's, Our Favorite Restaurant in Town*


I'm lying down now, solo on a couch,
imagining along with the music
that if I were, say, 15 or 16 tonight
and in possession of a fresh can
of pink or orange spray paint,
I would climb the 4th Street overpass
and write in big letters
HANK MOBLEY SWINGS
for all to see on their morning drive to work.

But having sailed some time ago
into the quiet cardigan harbor of my life,
out of earshot of the siren songs
that lure men onto reefs of foolishness
not to mention the bridges of bravado,
it's enough to let the soap bubble
of that Hank Mobley thought drift slowly
across the living room and burst
with no warning, much to the amazement of the cat.

## The Card Players

I'm glad Cézanne was not here in Key West
to set up an easel, and paint
the card game I was in last night,
unless he was really good at depicting despondency.

Cézanne once said that a single carrot,
if painted in a completely fresh way,
would be enough to set off a revolution.
I'll bet he was sitting in a café that day

where such observations are usually made,
but if I had been sitting in that café
across from Cézanne, I would have quipped,
"Maybe if Bugs Bunny were in charge of things,"

and I would have described in a fresh way
how the famous rabbit might be portrayed
using a carrot to point the mob to the Bastille.

Beer and chips and more beer and chips
were served at the poker table,
but no carrot soup, a staple on every menu
in the bunny rabbit stories of Beatrix Potter

and a dish that would have warmed me
inside and out the way a good soup does
and made me feel much better
about losing all my money and then some.

But at least now I have found the answer
to the old question of who would you invite
to your ideal dinner party:
Paul Cézanne, Bugs Bunny, Beatrix Potter,
and okay, maybe at the last minute, Gore Vidal.

# Vivace!

*No man is lonely while eating spaghetti.*
—CHRISTOPHER MORLEY

This time, I was at a corner table at Pasta Vivace!
on that side street next to the old music store.
The place was not at all crowded.
Just enough young men and women
were coming and going to keep me
occupied as I sipped my Campari and soda
and waited for the waiter to arrive with my pasta.

I imagined what the parents of all these people
were doing this evening,
then I thought of all of the diners as babies
with looks of amazement on their tiny faces.
Then as they kept arriving and departing,
holding the door for one another,
they turned into skeletons in their caskets,

each being carried by six husky pallbearers,
who would also be dead by now,
as I would be before too long,
for death is the magnetic north of poetry.

But first, I must insist on having the pleasure

of eating my *linguini con vongole,*

dipping chunks of crusty bread into the briny sauce,


for this is also a poem about happiness,

a celebration of the senses

and of all the men and women coming and going.

And if you turn your head a little this way,

you can see me at a corner table,

twirling the pasta with a fork and spoon

like an infant with a bib tucked under his chin.

## A Terrible Beauty

> *April is the cruelest month . . .*
> —T. S. ELIOT

If you happened to miss this year's
Cruelest Month Competition,
it began with all twelve contestants
taking the stage together
in the order of the calendar year,
each dressed in outfits
that sang of their personalities—
March windblown and wet with rain,
October resplendent in red and orange.

Many wondered why April, a perennial loser,
would even bother to show up,
always smiling, daffodils
embroidered on her bodice.
Some blamed it on a poem she'd read somewhere.

Others followed her early elimination—
August with zinc slathered on her nose,
December looking like the Mother of God.

It must be said that no one was surprised
when the tuxedoed man with the microphone
finally announced this year's winner,
the same as every year since its beginning.

Even though she'd shivered
during the swimsuit part
and stumbled when asked
how she planned to change the world,
February was the obvious choice.
*I mean the Super Bowl's over by then*
*and spring's a mile away.*
*What could be crueler?* as one guy put it.
And that was about it, except for the coronation.

There she stood, the only month on the stage,
crying a few chilly tears,
a thin smile frozen on her lips.
Then she bent her knees a little
so as to be less tall,
and some official placed on her head
her latest dripping, silvery crown of ice.

## Duck Blind

The idea behind a duck blind
is that any duck flying over it

will be blind to its existence,
seeing (or not seeing in the case of the duck)

how well the blind was camouflaged
with branches and leaves

to fit in with its natural surroundings.
Ignorant of the blind, a duck

has a better shot of being shot,
then tumbling out of the sky,

wing over useless wing,
only to land in the reeds of a marsh,

a clump of plumage now,
blind to everything, and deaf, too,
to the barking of the wet dogs,
to more gunfire later in the morning,

and to the soft talk of the hunters
waiting there, concealed by the blind.

## She's Gone

leaving me here alone again,
feeling this time
like one of those pairs of drawings
featured in the colorful puzzle section
of the Sunday paper,
where you have to detect
the barely detectable differences between the two.

Needless to say,
I am the drawing on the right
where items are found to be missing—
the guitar now down to four strings,
the bouquet with one flower gone,
the teacup minus its handle,
no longer able to be gracefully raised.

That's the new me—
no more sweet tunes, perfume, or chamomile.

And then there is the milking stool
where the farmer used to sit
every morning and evening
squeezing the milk from his herd.

But one of its legs is absent now,

and the farmer has toppled over

in his straw hat and overalls,

only to land beneath

the poor brindled cow in the drawing,

now minus a mark from her flank

and all four of her munificent udders erased.

# Downpour

Last night we ended up on the couch
trying to remember
all of the friends who had died so far,

and this morning I wrote them down
in alphabetical order
on the flip side of a shopping list
you had left on the kitchen table.

So many of them had been swept away
as if by a hand from the sky,
it was good to recall them,
I was thinking
under the cold lights of a supermarket
as I guided a cart with a wobbly wheel
up and down the long, strident aisles.

I was on the lookout for blueberries,
English muffins, linguini, heavy cream,
light bulbs, apples, Canadian bacon,
and whatever else was on the list,
which I managed to keep grocery side up,

until I had passed through the electric doors,
where I stopped to realize,
as I turned the list over,
that I had forgotten Terry O'Shea
as well as the bananas and the bread.

It was pouring by then,
spilling, as they say in Ireland,
people splashing across the lot to their cars.

And that is when I set out,
walking slowly and precisely,
a soaking-wet man
bearing bags of groceries,
walking as if in a procession honoring the dead.

I felt I owed this to Terry,
who was such a strong painter,
for almost forgetting him
and to all the others who had formed
a circle around him on the screen in my head.

I was walking more slowly now
in the presence of the compassion
the dead were extending to a comrade,

plus, I was in no hurry to return
to the kitchen, where I would have to tell you
all about Terry and the bananas and the bread.

# Three

## Safe Travels

Every time Gulliver travels
into another chapter of *Gulliver's Travels*
I marvel at how well traveled he is
despite his incurable gullibility.

I don't enjoy traveling anymore
because, for instance,
I still don't know the difference
between a *bloke* and a *chap*.

And I'm embarrassed
whenever I have to hold out a palm
of loose coins to a cashier
as if I were feeding a pigeon in a park.

Like Proust, I see only trouble
in store if I leave my room,
which is not lined with cork,
only sheets of wallpaper

featuring orange flowers
and little green vines.
Of course, anytime I want
I can travel in my imagination

but only as far as Toronto,

where some graduate students

with goatees and snoods

are translating my poems into Canadian.

## Hawaii

As you and I walked
through the palm forest of W. S. Merwin,
our guide was telling us how it began
in an abandoned pineapple grove
and that the soil, now without nutrients,
had to be revived before anything would grow.

The palms came from all over the world,
he said, and anyone who worked here
had to know their Latin names by heart.
The immense forest was hard to see
for the ranks of individual trees.
But back home, this morning, you can't miss

the four Chinese-red pots on the back deck
with the young palms sprouting
from the seeds you picked up
from the litter of seeds on the forest floor,
the ones you showed me on our flight home,
wrapped up like little mummies in paper towels.

This is not how the pig got his curly tail

or how the zebra got its stripes,

but it is how we happen to have some of the work

of W. S. Merwin growing here in Florida

in addition to his other major works

lined up in some rough order on a high shelf inside.

## The Emperor of Ice Cubes

Three small, nondescript shorebirds,
probably sandpipers,
investigating a clump of dry seaweed
in the tideline,
another one racing
along the water's shifting edge,
legs, thin as pencil lead,
scissoring back and forth in the wet sand.

I might have left it at that,
a beachgoer's morning take,
if an ice cube I tossed
hadn't landed near them
and if one of them did not start
pecking and even sipping at it,
while rebuffing the others
if they neared this prize in the sand.

What would a pecking bird
make of this frozen curio
beyond something cold to peck at?
Did it fall from outer space?
Would it remind the bird

of its second home in the Arctic,
where sandpipers migrate
flying mostly by night,
with lots of ice to peck at on arrival?
Imagine—a bird missing the cold
while pecking at an ice cube
as it melted in the Florida sand.

In the end, it hardly mattered
if or what the bird was thinking.
The bottled beer in the Igloo cooler,
source of the magical cube,
where many other ice cubes
lay gathered, was still very cold.
And it all seemed framed for me,
this bigger seascape,
when I leaned back to look—
nothing but pale blue sky,
clouds pushed around in the wind,
and bright white waves
rolling over one another,
then breaking on the sand.

# I Am Not Italian

I am not Italian, technically speaking,
yet here I am leaning on a zinc bar in Perugia
on a sunny weekday morning,
my foot up on the worn iron railing
just like the other men who,
it must be said, are officially and fully Italian.

It's 8:40 and they are off to work,
some in offices, others sweeping the streets
while I am off to a museum or a church
to see paintings, maybe light a candle in an alcove.
Yet here we all are in our suits and work shirts
joined in the brotherhood of espresso,

or how is it said? *La fratellanza dell'espresso,*
draining our little white cups
with an artful rotation of the wrist,
each of us tasting the same sweetness of life,
if you take a little sugar, and the bitterness
of its brevity, whether you choose to take sugar or not.

## The Symphony Orchestra of San Miguel de Allende

The Symphony Orchestra of San Miguel de Allende
is not made up of the usual instruments.

Instead of brass, strings, and woodwinds,
there are church bells, roosters, doves, and barking dogs,
all of which predate the horn, the violin, and the oboe,
notably the rooster, who crowed even before the time of Christ.

The orchestra plays all day and into the night,
but the music is most alive in the early morning
when much of the audience is half asleep
and not distracted by their jobs
and errands as they will be later in the day.

At first, as I listened from my canopied bed,
it sounded like a jumble of noise
until I imagined a gigantic score
written centuries ago by the Mozart of Mexico,

the genius who decided those dogs should come in
just after the thirty-two gongs of a solemn bell,
who had the doves modulate into an adagio,
and who added a rest here and there
where the roosters should pause, but not for long.

Are we not seekers of order, I thought,
as when we follow the lines in our palms
or connect the dots of the stars to form a bear in the sky?

So before rising from our slumberous beds,
why not listen a little longer
to this composition for dogs, roosters, doves, and bells?

The dogs are barking to be fed.
The roosters are beckoning us to the henhouse
where three eggs are still warm in the straw.
But the doves are mourning our awful losses,
and the bells are there to remind us of God.

## Dublin

So much to be viewed out here in the drizzle
with all the tall buses swinging themselves
so close to me around corners and men
in bunches smoking outside the betting parlors.

And when the rain falls steadily enough
to drive me into a gallery or a city castle,
then the learning also comes pouring down
whether I am in the mood for it or not.

Today, it's the codex of Leonardo on display
in the dim light where you touch a screen
to turn a page, the margins busy with pulleys
and siphons, whirlwinds, tides, and sluices.

And better informed was I to read on a little card
the news that Herbert Hoover translated
into English for the first time the works
of Agricola, the father of modern mineralogy himself.
Out the windows of the gallery,
a jumble of raincoats and black umbrellas,
and so my afternoon education continues
with the discovery in a vitrine of Vegetius,

who in the fifth century came up
with the idea of underwater warfare,
hand-to-hand combat beneath the lily pads
as if bloodying one another on the ground were not enough.

And if his illustration of an armed soldier
standing on the bottom of a lake
and breathing through a snake-like tube
comes at me tonight and shakes me out of sleep,

I will not coax an oval pill from its bottle
nor put on a robe and stand by the stove
looking at the ads in a magazine
while some milk is heating in a pan.

I only need to slide into place
the image of Leonardo at a table by a window,
his marvelous head resting in his hands,
wondering if water might exist on the moon.

## Cremation

It's half the binary of fire or earth,
but the question of where one's ashes
will go has many more answers than two.

Scattering is the option *du jour,*
maybe over a favorite body of water—
a lake where she learned to fish,
an ocean he liked to stare into toward the end.

Others pick multiple locations—
a ballpark, a backyard,
a rose garden, and the roof of a gym.
And guess who's not here to divide
the nearly weightless powder into equal parts?

Shake your heads, but bear in mind
that without a wish
you could end up in a coffee can
on a high shelf, your widow glancing up—
but not frequently enough—from an armchair.

I've always thought "hither and thither"
would make things easy on my survivors,
who would dither, then laughing toss
handfuls of me from a speeding convertible.

But wouldn't the easiest spot of all be
the nearby fireplace or Franklin stove,
where I, who enjoyed walking
amid the yellow-green trees of spring
or the bare, crisscross branches of winter,

would at last be indistinguishable
from the cinders of the maple,
the mighty oak, and even the pale mountain ash.

Now, I'm not sure how you heard it,
but in my version, Bob Hope's wife
asked her husband on his deathbed
whether he wanted to be buried or cremated.
"Surprise me," replied the comic before expiring.

## Lakeside Cottage: Ontario

When I mentioned to you on the phone
that I had just witnessed a flock of Canada geese
flying in a V only a few feet above the surface of the lake,
you asked if I had taken a picture.
I told you no, because the phone was up to my ear
as I waited for you to answer and also because
it rarely occurs to me to take a picture of anything.
So let me make a picture of the geese for you now.

There were at least thirty of them, appearing
quite suddenly, just after I dialed your number,
from behind the trees by the shore,
now heavy with the greenery of midsummer,

and they flew from right to left
like a text written in Hebrew,
almost touching the slightly ruffled water
as they passed by the dock at the end of the lawn.

You know, the dock with the little flight of stairs
that disappears into the lake, which made it easier
for your parents to go in for a swim
in the cold water before they both died

only months apart, as if Jack followed Mary's lead.
Otherwise, they might be sitting here now
in the two chairs by the picture window,
maybe holding cups of morning coffee,

as all the geese sailed by, heading who knows where,
so close to the water, each holding its position,
the leader pointing the way with its neck
extended, as if he were pulling the others along.

## The Convergence of My Parents

This morning I am looking out my window
at a crowd of white irises,
imagining that I am my mother in 1934
looking out the window of her train,
the one she rode from Toronto to Los Angeles
to work as a nurse in Queen of Angels Hospital,
only her train has stopped outside a little town
somewhere in the Midwest,
and she is looking out at the irises in someone's garden.

Around that time, maybe my young father
from Massachusetts was riding
another train from Boston to Galveston
to work as an electrician on an offshore oil rig,
a man who was more likely to be reading a newspaper
than admiring the flowers in a stranger's garden
but who must have spent some time
looking out at the scenery, wondering about himself,
and maybe a field of wildflowers went flashing by.

I wouldn't be here looking at irises
or anything else had they not found each other years later,
the nonparallel lines of their lives meeting in New York,

where I was born because I wanted to be close
to my mother, my father liked to joke.
She was still a nurse, and he was her patient.
He had been struck on the forehead by a tool
a co-worker had mishandled, and that is the story
of how I got here, how I pulled out of the first station of my life.

## Dreaming of the Middle Ages

I've never laid eyes on a church mouse,
but I know what it is to be as poor as a graduate student,
for I spent many semesters
drinking discount beer
and eating a concoction
topped with melted cheese and hot sauce
that was known at the time as Kansas City Rice.

I was studying to be a medievalist,
and I often fell asleep in an armchair
with a book still open on my lap
whose margins were crowded
with coded notations regarding
*Beowulf, The Mabinogion,*
*Piers Ploughman,* or *Sir Gawain and the Green Knight.*

I wouldn't say I was eating and breathing
the literature of the Middle Ages,
because, in fact, I was eating Kansas City Rice
and breathing in pack after pack of Marlboro Reds.

Yet these old tales and romances
followed me in my waking hours
and did not hesitate to enter my dreams.

This was in Southern California,
and my bedroom was suffused
with the perfume of the nearby orange groves.
There, I dallied with the Wife of Bath
and rode along with the Parson and the Prioress.

On one of these nights,
I even had a showdown with Sir Gawain himself,
the two of us facing off
in a large mead hall full of boisterous guests.

I had somehow sullied his honor,
and before I could utter a word of apology,
with one mighty swing Gawain passed his sword
through my middle, cutting me precisely in two.

A raucous cheer went up from the crowd
as my upper half toppled to the floor with a sick thud.

Some of the knights and ladies stood
in a circle around what was left of me,
examining the many tree rings
now visible in my exposed lower half,

while they stroked their chins
and marveled over the many rings
that represented my years in graduate school.

Yes, that was a big chunk of my life,
and even though I've quit the cigarettes
and I eat a lot better these days,
often in candlelight with a loving woman,

I still write in the margins of books,
and in my dreams I still chase a rabbit
with a ribbon tied around his neck
up and down the endless lanes of an orange grove,
pursued in turn by Grendel and his blood-caked mother.

## The Yellow Wood

Two roads diverged in a yellow wood,
then those two roads diverged again
and kept diverging the way branches
diverge into more branches to form a tree,
which you fall out of one day and die.

It's troubling to think of life that way,
as a series of binary choices,
each one leaving behind a road forsaken.
No, you can't go down two at a time
and be both tailor and candlestick maker.

But you're free to dream of the other.
Take this poet, elbows on the sill,
imagining my life as a baker or even a tinker,
that is, *a person who goes from place to place*
[though I've grown weary of traveling]

*mending metal utensils on his way,*
as if the people who compiled
this dictionary had the foggiest idea
what tinkering actually demanded—
what solitude and hardship such a life must entail!

## My Funeral

After the eulogies and this and that
and a blessing
and whatever follows,
as pedestrians outside walk along
under the leaning steeple
on their way to this place or that,
there will come a moment
when everyone will have had quite enough.

Then the fox will tap
a music stand with his bow
and lift his violin,
and the badgers will raise their horns
to their snarling badger lips,
ready to play what is required,
and the bear will gently set
his paws upon the upright bass.

And their playing will accompany everyone
down the aisle and outdoors
into the weather of the day,
whatever it may be,
and down a block or two south,

then around a corner to a bar
with a neon beer sign in the window.

And its interior will be a greeting,
full of blue shadows
with a streak of late-morning light,
so that everyone is glad to be alive
and sorry I couldn't be there,
and it's even okay
that the bartender turns out to be a horse.

And as for me,
gliding off into space,
all I would ask as my final wish
is that you refrain, out of respect,
from shouting over the heads of the others,
now two or three deep at the bar,
"When did the cow sell this place?"

Wait your turn, then order up.
Today is no different in that regard.

## The Pregnant Man

A man is pregnant.
He doesn't know that he's pregnant
but unlike the other men wearing caps
at a shady table outside a café,
he wants to give birth
to something that is alive

even if it's only a short poem
breathing in and out,
a girl poem or a boy poem,
it wouldn't matter to his mighty love.
Look at him now playing cards
while the old waiter goes about his business.

## Architecture at 3:30 A.M.

Brunelleschi
is asleep
in Florence.
Christopher Wren
is snoring
in a corner of London.
Louis Sullivan
is curled up
somewhere
in Chicago.
Only Dagwood is
awake at this hour
in his bathrobe
in the kitchen,
refrigerator door open,
a pickle jar
under one arm,
the mayonnaise
balanced
on a free elbow,
about to construct
another phenomenal
tower of a sandwich.

I don't care that no one
under 55 will know
who Dagwood is,
and no one over 55
will remember him.
Dagwood is still
standing in
the Bumstead kitchen,
bathed in refrigerator light,
knowing his hunger
will be appeased
but not before
he labors, along with all
the other geniuses,
under gravity's singular law.

## The Garland

I would like to be laid to rest in a big tomb
topped by a stone figure of an angel,
who appears to have landed there
in order to sob forevermore,
her face buried in her bent arm,
one folded wing hanging by her side.

Then, whenever I found the time
to visit my own grave,
after approaching with slow, respectful steps,
I would place around her rough neck
the garland of wildflowers that I knitted,
then run back to the car, laughing and immortal!

# Four

## Me First

We often fly in the sky together,
and we're always okay—there's our luggage now
waiting for us on the carousel.

And we drive lots of places
in all manner of hectic traffic,
yet here we are, pulling in the driveway again.

So many opportunities to die together,
but no meteor has hit our house,
no tornado has lifted us into its funnel.

The odds say then that one of us will go
before the other, like heading off
into a heavy snowstorm, leaving

the other one behind to stand in the kitchen
or lie on the bed under the fan.
So why not let me, the older one, go first?

I don't want to see you everywhere
as I wait for the snow to stop,
before setting out with a crooked stick, calling your name.

# A Sight

Last night I watched a documentary on war,
and the part I carry with me today
is the spectacle of a line
of maybe twenty blinded soldiers
being led, single file
away from a yellow cloud of gas.

That might be what accounts
for this morning's brightness—
sunlight slathered over everything
from the royal palms to the store awnings,
from a blue Corolla at the curb
to a purple flower climbing a fence,
one gift of sight after another.

I couldn't see their bandaged faces,
but each man had one hand
resting on the shoulder
of the man in front of him,
so that every man was guiding
and being guided at the same time,
and in the same tempo,
given the unison of their small, cautious steps.

## Air Sax

In the dorm rooms of our snowbound college
during certain parts of the Coltrane solos
featured on the album *Milestones,*
parts we had deemed exceedingly worthy,
we boys would play imaginary
tenor saxophones by placing a thumb
in our mouths, leaving the free hand
to handle the intricacies of the fingering,

and with puffed-out cheeks and eyes closed,
we would blow hard, instead of sucking
as we had done in our infancy.
And even though we would step back
to laugh at the silly pathos of ourselves,
there was always great intensity and joy in our playing.

## English Roses

In those weeks of late summer
when the roses in gardens begin to fade,
the big red, white, and pink ones—
the inner enfolded petals growing cankerous,
the petals at the edges turning brown
or fallen already down on their girlish backs
in the rough beds of turned-over soil,

then how terrible the expressions on their faces,
a kind of was-it-all-really-worth-it look,
to die here in front of everybody
in the garden of a bed-and-breakfast
in a provincial English market town,
to expire by degrees of corruption
in plain sight of all the neighbors passing by—

the thin mail carrier, the stocky butcher
(thank God the children pay no attention),
the swiveling faces in the windows of the tall buses,
and now this stranger staring over the wall,
hair disheveled, a loose scarf around his neck,
jotting in a notebook, something about us no doubt,
about how terrible we must look now under the punishing sun.

## On the Deaths of Friends

Either they just die
or they get sick and die of the sickness
or they get sick, recover, then die of something else,
or they get sick, appear to recover,
then die of the same thing,
the sickness coming back
to take another bite out of you
in the forest of your final hours.

And there are other ways,
which will not be considered here.
In the evening, I closed my eyes
on the shore of a lake and I pretended
this is what it will look like
or will not look like,
this is where my friends keep going,
a "place" only in quotation marks,

where, instead of oxygen, there is silence
unbroken by the bark of a fox in winter
or the whistle of a neglected kettle.
With eyes still closed,
I ran in the dark toward that silence,

like a man running along a train platform,
and when I opened my eyes to see
who was running in the other direction

with outspread arms,
there was the lake again with its ripples,
a breeze coming off the water,
and a low train whistle,
and there was I trembling
under the trees, passing clouds,
and everything else that was pouring
over the mighty floodgates of the senses.

## Cupid

Fresh in from the rain,
you asked me
how long a cubit is.

I thought
the subject at hand
was love.

But it was an ark
you were building,
a little one, just for you.

## Talking to Myself

When I talk to myself,
as I sit in a chair or pace the floor,
I don't bother to listen,
because my hearing is so bad
I wouldn't be able to pick out a word,
plus I have nothing new to say.

The sound of my voice was a comfort
when I used to sit by my bedside
reading to myself one animal fable
after another until the words
became the vowels of a lullaby
and I vanished under the blanket of sleep.

As a boy, I talked to each mailbox
I passed on my bicycle, a black Humber,
made in England, it said on the frame.
I would pedal around the neighborhood,
sitting up tall, arms hanging limp,
looking for the street that would lead to England.

I'm not alone in talking to myself.
Children sit alone on a carpet,
talking to their imaginary friends.
The elderly keep gabbing in empty rooms.
A cow in a pasture is mooing to herself.
The skylark is singing pointlessly in the sky.

Down the street, a dog is barking all alone.
The cat remains silent with no one in mind.
And like her, I have been writing this
in silence, moving only my lips
over the words lined up in their pews,
but now I see I have gone and said them all to you.

# Ireland Floating on a Map of the World

With Lough Neagh serving as one eye,
the body of Ireland looks this morning
like nothing less than a rabbit or a hare
caught mid-flight in a mighty westward leap.

With the Ring of Kerry and Beara
as the springing hind legs
and jutting Mayo as its tender forepaws,
the rabbit, or again possibly a hare,

is turning his head to look back
at the middle part of Britain
around the Lake District, say, or Hadrian's Wall,
and thinking nothing but pleasant thoughts

about the America where he will eventually
land, for he is only famous for his leaping.

## The Flash Card

The real jazz insiders
like to refer to it as "the flash card,"
or if they don't, they should,
or at least they could come up with some name for it.
What is the matter with these people anyway?

Would it not help to have a term
to describe a sequence of notes
so brilliant that the rest of the solo
turns into wallpaper behind it
yet the musician absolutely refuses to repeat it?

He played it with such felicity
we know he could easily play it again,
passing the phrase through a ring of keys,
even cruising it around the circle of fifths,
but the man stone-cold refuses to give us another taste.

There's a name for that little indentation
between your upper lip and your nose
(I can't think of it right now)
and the Japanese have a special word
for the act of looking at cherry trees in bloom.

So why shouldn't we have a name for this?
"The Tease?" "The Now-You-See-It?"
Surely, there is room in the box of jive
for another bit of lingo.

Language belongs to its users, right?
Not to the professors and lexicographers
in their baggy jackets flecked with chalk dust.

How about it, people? Can you stop nodding
and drumming on the table with a swizzle stick?
Can we work as a team for once? Win one for Prez? For Bud?

*Anniversary*

The moment I turned a corner
into a quiet side street
of an unfamiliar city,

I ran into the realization
that you had died
exactly nine years ago today,

which led me to imagine a baby
born on the day you died,

a child who would always remain
the same age as your death
and whose birthday parties
would be secret memorials to you.

As time passed, more people
would meet this growing person,

but fewer and fewer people
would remember who you were

until one day when no one
would be alive
to remember you, not even me

or the make-believe boy
whom I contrived that day,

as my bicycle leaned against a tree
on a leafy side street,
somewhere in Philadelphia.

## Early People

Little is known about the Iberian people
called the Laietani
sounds like the unpromising beginning
of a term paper, does it not?
I'm guessing a C-minus at best.

But a better performance
than the paper that went:
Little is known about the writer Edgar Allan Poe,
for he left behind only his dates
which are Born 1809 Died 1849.
In conclusion, it's sad for anyone
to be dead for such a long time.

Teaching is a noble and time-honored profession,
but little is known about it
because no one is allowed in the classroom
except the teacher and the students.

The students don't take notes anymore,
and the teacher will forget everything
she said by lunchtime,

or she has been saying the same thing
for twenty or thirty years, or both.

Twenty or thirty years is not a long time
when you consider the Laietani people,
the smoke from whose fires rose
over the Iberian peninsula
even before the marauding Romans arrived
to give everyone an inferiority complex
with their alphabet, their aqueducts,
frigidaria, the important process of fermentation,
and their martial skills—
all those legions, phalanxes, vanguards, and catapults.

And that pretty much does it
regarding the Laietani,
although about the ancient Romans much is known,
too much to go into really
given the strict parameters of this assignment.

# My Father's Office, John Street, New York City, 1953

He would take me with him when I was a boy,
before it became a thing to do,
the two of us riding the subway,
then walking a few confining blocks
to the insurance company where he worked.

There, he would set me free to roam
up and down the long rows of typists,
clacking away on their manual machines,
fingernails red and hands blue
from the carbon paper, famous then
for working the miracle of triplicates.

The place was an Avalon of supplies—
reams of paper, envelopes neat in their boxes,
even a franking machine, your own private post office.
Sometimes I would stop to look down
on the wide expanse of New York Harbor,
never guessing how many of the office's
rituals and devices would soon disappear for good
into the gaping maw of obsolescence.

Now the oasis of the water cooler is gone,
and silenced is the aggregate racket of typing.

Blown away is the haze of smoke from cigarettes.
Gone, the ashtrays from every desk
and the tall ones by the elevators,
their sand kept smooth and clean
as if tended every night by a tiny man with a tiny rake.

No more thick tear-off calendars,
the days disappearing one page at a time.

No more fountain pen drawing
nectar from the black flower of an ink bottle.

No more black rotary phone,
ringing with good news, bad news, and worse.

Gone, the switchboard and the intercom,
the cable room, Rolodex, and Dictaphone.

Gone, too, the many paperweights,
which weighed down the stacks of papers,
so they wouldn't blow away
on a hot summer day with the windows wide open,
fans oscillating this way and that,

and men in shirtsleeves leaning
out high windows to catch a breeze.

Goodbye to the hat rack and the hats they held,
and gone the men themselves and gone my father,
gone my father as well.

Farewell, adding machine,
and the spindles where memos were impaled.
They went away while you were out.

But stay, oh paper clip,
and stay, too, rubber band,
keepers of order, logic, and sense
in the days of saloons and nightsticks,
evening editions, and newsreels

and still in these days when they both
dwell in the drawer of a worker
in a cubicle in a tower of glass.

She is bent over a glowing screen, her hand on a mouse
that she is using to download an elephant,
of all things, and to print out its picture in color,

the huge creature slipping through a wire
then materializing in her hand, a new miracle in triplicate.

## April 21st

It's the birthday of John Muir and Charlotte Brontë,
born just 18 years apart,
she in Yorkshire and he somewhere in Scotland,
both in their bassinets under the same grey clouds,
but then their lives diverge so wildly
you might question the claims of astrology,
if you haven't had the sense to do that already.

Muir heads off to Wisconsin (with his parents, I suppose),
whereas Charlotte is placed in a nearby boarding school.
Muir then stomps all over North America,
exulting in Nature and writing it all down,
while Charlotte stays mostly indoors, composing poems
with her sisters, Emily and Anne.
He leaves us *Picturesque California*, she *Jane Eyre*.

I don't have much on my calendar for today,
another April 21st featuring a walk around the lake,
then boxing up the cat and driving her to the vet.
It's overwhelming to think of all the things
I'm not doing today, including being born.
But I will say that my life, maybe like yours,
falls somewhere between John Muir's and Charlotte Brontë's.

My morning walk takes under an hour,

but I do pay attention to the water and the birds,

and here I am writing a poem, just like the Brontë sisters.

Muir was blinded for a spell,

Charlotte married then died still pregnant,

and I've had the same headache for more than a month.

And if that's what ends up killing me,

would someone please slide this poem

into a side pocket of the coat they bury me in?

Until then, let us picture John Muir

on a windy mountaintop in Oregon

waving in the direction of the coastal dunes,

while Charlotte Brontë lifts her head

from her morning prayers, remembering that it's her birthday.

## Massage

i

Face down
in that cushioned horseshoe,
the face cradle,
I watched her shoes appear, then disappear.

ii

Where else could you hear such music?
Unless you came across a waterfall
with a naked man
sitting under it playing the flute.

iii

The one in San Diego
could have been a kindly aunt
applying sunscreen to my back
when I was about four,
but I would have told
the one in Rochester every top secret
I knew and invented some others.

iv

While the right leg is being rubbed,
the left leg is thinking *I'm next*.


v

When I muttered *sorry*
for dozing off,
she said *no worries*.
She only minded
the crying, which more people do
than you would think when they are touched.


vi

When she lifted the sheet
for me to turn over,
it felt like a dream, or the afterlife.
A dream about the afterlife.


vii

Afterward,
I wanted to shake both
of her hands goodbye,
but one was occupied
with the offer of a paper cup of water.

## Hotel Rex

Looming over the little sewing kit
and the miniature bottles

of shampoo and conditioner,
I am a giant, a colossus,

a king standing before the royal mirror
in an enormous robe of terrycloth.

As a sign of my benevolence,
I will forego coffee,

scrambled eggs, and toast
from room service and check out early

before my tiny subjects arrive
to wash their hair and mend their simple attire.

## Going for a Walk as the Drugs Kick In

It's Friday, and the sun's all over everything
after a long week of steady rain.
The clouds have moved on
to hover over other counties.
The irises are showing their white faces
streaked with yellow and purple.
The bees are out again
making their floral visitations.
The beaver swims with a stick in his mouth.
The otter is looking out his window.
The butterfly doesn't seem to know where it's going.
So ample and worthy is the air around me,
I am only able to take in one bird at a time.
A fruit tree has started to sing.
The little town is farther away than ever.
I have my arm around the otter,
holding him by the shoulder.
The scene out his window is so plentiful
and everything is billowing with our love.

# Acknowledgments

Thanks to the editors of the following journals, where some of these poems first appeared:

*The Atlantic:* "Evening Wind," "I Am Not Italian," "Sleeping on My Side," "A Sight"

*Brilliant Corners:* "Air Sax," "The Flash Card," "Listening to Hank Mobley Around 11 O'Clock After a Long Fun Boozy Dinner, the Four of Us, at Captain Pig's, Our Favorite Restaurant in Town"

*Five Points:* "Imperial Garden," "The Symphony Orchestra of San Miguel de Allende," "Identity," "Walking My Seventy-Five-Year-Old Dog"

*The National:* "The Convergence of My Parents"

*New Ohio Review:* "April 21st," "The Card Players"

*The New Yorker:* "Downpour," "Safe Travels"

*The Paris Review:* "On the Deaths of Friends"

*Ploughshares:* "Hotel Rex"

*Plume:* "The Floors of Bonnard"

*Poetry East:* "The Garland," "And It's Raining Outside, Which Always Adds"

*The Southampton Review:* "Down on the Farm," "Irish Spider," "Prospect," "Life Expectancy," "Massage," "Me First," "Paris in May," "Whiskers"


"Contemporary Americans" appeared in *Off the Shelf: A Celebration of Bookshops in Verse,* ed. Carol Ann Duffy (Picador, New York, 2016), p. 14.

"My Father's Office, John Street, New York City, 1953," was commissioned by Xerox for an anthology of writing about the business office.

"The Garland" also appeared in *Lightning Strikes II,* an ekphrastic anthology (Dolby Chadwick Gallery, San Francisco, 2019).


Thanks are due to everyone at Random House who helped bring this book into being, especially my editor Ben Greenberg, Gina

Centrello, and the late Susan Kamil, who is deeply missed and fondly remembered here. Thanks also to my longtime agent, Chris Calhoun, for his steadfast advocacy and friendship. These poems were graded by George Green, my poetic conscience, who spared my readers anything lower than a B. And to Suzannah, much gratitude for her meticulous appraisals of my work and for agreeing to be my wife.

PHOTO: © SUZANNAH GAIL COLLINS

BILLY COLLINS is the author of thirteen collections of poetry including *Musical Tables, The Rain in Portugal, Aimless Love, Horoscopes for the Dead, Ballistics, The Trouble with Poetry, Nine Horses, Sailing Alone Around the Room, Questions About Angels, The Art of Drowning,* and *Picnic, Lightning.* He is also the editor of *Poetry 180: A Turning Back to Poetry, 180 More: Extraordinary Poems for Every Day,* and *Bright Wings: An Illustrated Anthology of Poems About Birds.* A former Distinguished Professor of English at Lehman College of the City University of New York, Collins served as Poet Laureate of the United States from 2001 to 2003 and as New York State Poet from 2004 to 2006. In 2016 he was inducted into the American Academy of Arts and Letters. He lives in Florida with his wife, Suzannah.

## ABOUT THE TYPE

The text of this book was set in Filosofia, a typeface designed in 1996 by Zuzana Licko, who created it for digital typesetting as an interpretation of the eighteenth-century typeface Bodoni, designed by Giambattista Bodoni (1740–1813). Filosofia, an example of Licko's unusual font designs, has classical proportions with a strong vertical feeling, softened by rounded droplike serifs. She has designed many typefaces and is the cofounder of *Emigre* magazine, where many of them first appeared. Born in Bratislava, Czechoslovakia, in 1961, Licko came to the United States in 1968. She studied graphic communications at the University of California, Berkeley, graduating in 1984.